Contents

0. Intro (Don't Skip Me!)

Hey friend. If you've picked up this book you are probably going through some shit right now, and for that I am so so sorry. When our worlds get rocked it is so hard to find which way is up, and even harder to figure out how to move towards grasping any image of progress. My hope and prayer is that through your reading experience you find comfort in knowing that you are not alone, so many have walked the rocky path before you, and you will, in fact, survive. Even more than that, you will flourish.

A little bit on my story—2015 and 2016 brought some of the biggest challenges I have ever encountered. Many issues came, but the most prominent were my parents separating out of nowhere, and the spiraling effect that had on my roundabout battle with severe depression. What a combo, right? I felt like every time I gained a little ground, hardship struck and the surface beneath my feet crumbled, leaving me all the way back where I started. With every step back Depression reared his head and taunted me with vicious thoughts of how incapable I was to handle the turmoil around me and reminders of the ways I *should* be operating (should is a mean little thing).

Through these challenges, it has been fascinating to reflect on the people that have come to my aid. Some come without expectations, simply showing up to be there and sit in the sadness alongside me. Others, with such good intentions, have brought their own experiences and expectations of mourning into the equation, adding pressure to the already heavy situation. I have gone back and forth on how to help those dealing with life-altering experiences and when led by the Holy Spirit, the outline for this book came together! Not only do I desire for the words in here to minister to those whose worlds have been rocked, but those who are supporting them as well. It takes a village, and I hope that by sharing my stories of pain and loss you will be able to see, in a new way, the deep, unique ways we as individuals experience anguish, and will be able to hold those around you in a new way.

There are going to be some choice words in here…. I am laying my whole self out and, on some days, that includes profanity. My dad living a double life and separating from my mom was absolute shit. Depression is the worst and on the really bad days, how do you think I felt? Lower than low. "Bad," "crappy," and "hard" just do. not. cut. it. I'm a firm believer that words only have the power we give them, and in this instance, I am using them as descriptors, not put downs or insults (though, that may come later). In this time of absolute change, I lost my endurance to try and live up to whatever standard of perfection was swirling in my mind, and this included my perfect way with words.

Hear my heart in this, friends—every single word in here is honest, vulnerable, and has been a risk for me to even write down. Including the "bad" ones. If this is an issue for you I would encourage you to put aside your skepticism or judgement and open your eyes while reading this book to see my pain and torment, in which these words make sense.

As you walk along the path you have been brought into, stumbled upon, or have come to as a result of your own actions, I pray and hope that you see me as a companion, knowing I have walked a similar one and am familiar with all its ins and outs. More than that, though, the biggest source of help you can reach out to is God, and His church. He is the only one that can be ever present with you in every facet of your experience.

There will be a multitude of emotions. There will be feelings you don't understand, waves of contradictory responses that come and go, leaving you confused and unsure of what to embrace and what to dismiss. Give yourself grace. Give yourself room to experience your feelings and handle them with friends, family, or experienced professionals. When we feel like everything is being Stripped, all bets are off.

I wish I could take you out for a cup of coffee, listen to you, cry with you, laugh with you, curse with you… just *be* with you in your pain. But because that's not always an option, I give you this book.

I pray you find hope through my story, grace for your own process, and, most of all, refuge in the God that makes redemption and reconciliation possible, even in the most hopeless of situations. Let's dive in.

May the God of hope fill you with all joy and peace as you trust in him, so that you may overflow with hope by the power of the Holy Spirit.

Romans 15:13

(This was Paul's desire for his church, and it's my prayer for you, too)

1. The Night My Reality Crumbled

9.3.15
1:30am

Oh Lord.
What? Like what the hell. I come home and find out
my dad is leaving for a few nights. There are so
many things I am grateful for about this situation,
but man it hurts. I feel like my dad is an enemy.
Like he lied. We. Don't. Do. This. in our family.
This doesn't happen. Did he cheat? Does he have a
problem? Oh Lord do not allow our family to fall.
DO NOT allow my parents marriage to fall. Jesus,
save us. Save us, Father. I am scared. Will
everything be different? I don't want to hate him.
Oh God, thinking about what he said to me and how
he hugged me… This is hard for him too. Don't
allow me to see only the sin or only the hard stuff.

Please Jesus, restore my relationship with my dad. I don't want to lose him. I don't want to be mad at him or not be able to trust him. So many emotions. SO. MANY. EMOTIONS. Jesus, I feel like things will never be the same. I am so scared that everything I've ever known about marriage and family is ruined. The way my mom was talking about how events progressed sounded like some other family, not mine. I don't even know. Jesus I want everything and everyone to be happy and able to communicate, but obviously that's not gonna happen. Help me Father. Calm me down. Take these swirling emotions and sift through them with me. I can't do this alone. I NEED you. Come through for me. For us.
-M

It was a Thursday night, I was leaving school after a science lab and texted my mom that I was coming home. Texting her wasn't a usual thing, but she asked me to let her know when I was on my way because people were coming over. I thought nothing of it and got in my car, drove home and arrived to find my mom on the patio with her Bible study friends. It was odd that they were over when she had only mentioned that the men of the study would be over with my dad, but I decided to just wave "hello" and go to my room. She motioned for me to come outside. As I went, she came up to me and wrapped me in an unusually big hug. I figured she was just showing off her mom skills to her church friends until she pulled away, grabbed my hands, and said, "I need to talk to you."

Let me back up a little. Growing up, there were a lot of deaths in the family—an unusual amount of death for a person my age to experience. From grandparents and young cousins, to random older relatives, my twin sister, Megan, and I were familiar with funerals by the time we reached fifth grade. We had an inside joke—that really isn't funny at all when you think about it—whenever we got called up to the office at school, the office ladies would say, "Your mom told me to tell you that nobody died." That being said, you can imagine the sheer anxiety that pulsed through my every vein

when I caught onto my mom's strange actions.
Back to the patio—

I went cold and asked blankly, "What happened." She just kept saying that she needed to talk to me and took me inside the house. At this point, one of our pastors, Heidi, walked into the room and I went into full panic mode. Who died. It had to be pretty bad if all these people, and Heidi, the Communications and Crisis pastor of our church, were here on such short notice. I began asking over and over where Dad was until I saw him in the living room and breathed a deep sigh of relief. He was wearing grey sweats, white socks, and the worn-out mustard sweatshirt he always wore. I brushed off my panic and laughed, wiped invisible sweat off my forehead and then noticed another pastor, Stan, walk in the room.

My dad brought me in for a tight side hug. Our conversation went like this:

Me: "What's wrong?"

Him: "I have to think about some things and pray about some things, and fall on my face before God, and to do that I can't be home right now."

Me:

"...........................what................."

I didn't hug him back. I stood stiff and limp all at the same time. I didn't see his face because he turned and left swiftly. I didn't have a clue what was happening. Looking back on it now, I think he hugged me so incredibly tight because he knew that when I knew why he was leaving, he wouldn't be hugging me for a very, very long time.

Up to this point I had experienced loss, but not in a life-altering way. Growing up my family was close. My parents were leaders in the church, and I found pieces of my identity in the way they were sacredly, or more accurately, *perfectly*, put together. Walking into an emotional, relational ground zero left me gasping for air and reaching for normalcy. What I knew as normal was long gone.

This enormous blow left my mind reeling and my body in shock. I burst into tears with no connection to any emotion. I physically reacted to the intake of information that my mind could not hold.

When struck with traumatic news that has no place in our normal reality, our minds use every fiber of their being to make sense of the information and place it in actuality, lining up with events and memories surrounding the revelation. This function is helpful in normal life when sensible conclusions can be easily reached. However, when the information being taken in is wildly unexpected and contradictory to the understood reality, this reaction is *exhausting.*

When my brain tried to put this square
information into my circular reality I felt like I was
going crazy. I had known that feeling before when I
was dealing with undiagnosed depression, but this
craziness was faster, with thoughts and memories
zipping past my grasp.

After I caught my breath, I retreated into the
kitchen to get some water. Heidi was in there and
after talking for a few moments I sighed and rolled
out my feelings in the statement, "This is *so*
embarrassing." Heidi met my eyes and spoke to my
soul, in the way that only she can, by responding,
"This is *not* your shame to bear." As a recovering
people pleaser, it was easy for me to take on the
fault in any situation and attempt to figure out a way
to make it better so everyone would be happy again.
In recovery, this is referred to as co-dependence.
With the waves of sin and division crashing on me
over and over, my natural tendency was to find the

problem and fix it, while also over-analyzing my feelings so they would fit into the little "this is how to perfectly function" box I had created. Issues would arise in this mindset when problems became my task and I was unable to immediately fix them perfectly. Whether you find this crazy or relate to it on a deep level, this was a fact of my reality. When faced with the weight of my dad's then unknown actions and my inability to make sense of them, I was swept up by a strong, deteriorating sense of shame.

Though I wasn't aware of it, my mind connected my dad's actions with my actions as a daughter, and human being. My role as a functioning individual *should have* been enough to stop my dad from going down the path that he did, but as we both know, that is not the truth. As we both know, that wouldn't have prevented anything.

I know I am not responsible for my father's actions.
I did not cause my dad to step into, and then be
completely consumed by sin. I know I was a great
daughter, and a pretty rad person overall. Though
my "performance" in life was technically more than
sufficient, it had nothing to do with my dad's
choices. When prompted by lust and temptation, he
took the first step away from doing right and in turn
slipped down a slope into the depths of deep
remorse that only God himself could save him from.
When shame sets in the effect can be so gripping, so
invasive, overstepping all boundaries and
infiltrating every aspect of your being. Knowing
that the situation at hand is not your fault does not
always alleviate the pressure coming at you from
the inside out.

This night changed my life. My thoughts,
feelings, actions, emotions, were *all* impacted by
just a few short hours that uncovered years of

destructive sin. This night, and many nights to follow, were abundantly heavy, with information of past and present coming to light, weighing down my soul. I felt like I had no hope. I tried to talk myself off the ledge of "What is truth?" but with streams of thought surging in every direction and crashing into each other, my understanding of life and relationship were completely overturned.

Joy felt far beyond grasp. The thought of having a functioning "family" like I had known was obliterated. Anger boiled within me— my world was rocked, my normalcy was shattered, and my reality was jagged and rough, completely Stripped.

My dad was unfaithful to my mom. In his sinfulness, in his selfishness, he destroyed the life and family that the two of them had worked so hard to build over their twenty-year relationship.

The foundations of my very being seemed to have been slashed, trampled on, uprooted and ripped to shreds. While this was utterly excruciating, there were small flickers of hope, small reminders that this was not a permanent reality.

One absolutely beautiful element of the worst night of my life thus far, possibly the only beauty of that evening, was the people that were there for us in the midst of such despair. Heidi and the Bible study peeps held us in our pain and confusion. I called my friends in anguish and they sped to my side. Stan and his wife drove to Los Angeles to pick up my sister from school and bring her home so we could all be together.

They didn't make us talk.

They didn't step on our anguish with clichés or premature pictures of a happy ending.

They sat and waited on us to set the tone for their support. They didn't finish our sentences or even quote scripture—they *lived* it in how they embraced us.

The way they showed up for us spoke the truth and love of God. They relied on God to lead and guide and took hold of their role as a tangible example of His presence, stepping into our pain and holding us tightly when we needed stability.
This is the Bride of Christ in action. This is the Church, embracing sinners and those wounded by sin with love and grace. And while Mom, Megan and I were being held in our anguish, my dad was being met with truth.

Unbeknownst to me, the week leading up to this was one filled with hard conversations and truth coming to light. The grace and love we received was only able to come once sin was exposed, truth was spoken and the problem at hand was faced, head on. This was only the first step in a long journey of decisions, actions, and consequences.

The night ended, with bleak potential for the success of our family. The only hope we had was the thought of new information coming into play and helping us understand the absurdity surrounding us. Tylenol PM put our minds to rest as we went to bed with no idea of what was to come. I journaled for the last time before a two-year break, as bearing so much pain took the slightest sliver of vulnerability and left my emotions everywhere— each small issue building up into an immovable mountain. I closed my book of thoughts in anger and anguish, praying through my journaling that I would make it through the obviously rugged road that lay before me. Sleep came slowly. My eyes blinked closed as my mind faded to stillness, though slumber was close rest was far far away.

In hindsight, I love the image that comes to mind when I think about God saving my dad from the deepest, loneliest, most shameful time of his life. This image is similar to what comes to mind when I think about my own salvation and the relational love God has for all his creation. I picture a little child being stuck—whether in a muddy mess or a tight car seat. What do children do when they need help? They cry and they raise their arms to their mamas and daddies. This image perfectly portrays the first step to recovery of any kind—submission to those that can help, with the acknowledgement that we need it.

I feel like it's so common for people to make jokes about that friend we all have who is *really* into coffee, shopping, Greys Anatomy, etc. by saying, "You know, acceptance is the first step to recovery." While this use of the phrase is laid back and light hearted, the truth of the matter remains. Acceptance of the situation we find ourselves in is the first step towards progress. The second? Deciding you want to change it.

Even if you aren't having to accept a situation caused by your own actions, humans have to make the choice: to come to terms with what is reality, or to deny what is going on around you, and therefore deny opportunity for growth. Look around, see where you're at, especially when you feel like the truth of the circumstances might crush you. After that? Lift your arms to your heavenly daddy. I'm not a big fan of calling God daddy, but father is just too formal sometimes. Reach up with both hands, leaving the mess you've created, or have been brought into, behind, and wait on your daddy to come pick you up and clean you off. You can choose to stay in the mess, whining about being there, disgusted by the situation before you, or you can grab onto the One who can bring you out of it.

The shame you feel, whether warranted or created in your mind, was taken and paid for at the cross and that is where it can stay. There is a difference between *adjusting* to a rocked world, and *remaining* in the wreckage.

One of my favorite articulations of this concept is by Jen Sincero in her masterpiece of a book, *You Are a Badass.* She says, "It's not your fault that you're fucked up, but it's your fault if you stay fucked up."[1] My world was absolutely shaken by someone else's actions. The mess was not made by me, but it was my choice to stay in it or be motivated by it. I chose to fight for healing, because healing and recovery are just that—a fight.

---

[1] Jen Sincero, *You are a Badass: How to Stop Doubting Your Greatness and Start Living an Awesome Life*. 2013.

The choice is yours, friend. What choice will you make today? It's not an easy one by any means, but it's *yours*. Own it. Guard it. Fight for it. Grab someone that cares about you, reflect on what you need, and step on the path towards healing. This is not a lighthearted encouragement, I have walked the path and I *know* it's treacherous. You decide when your healing starts, why wait another moment? Even when you feel absorbed by death, choose life. Choose grace. Choose hope. Grip tight to goodness and don't let it go. On some days my only smile came from a silly Netflix show, or a delicious chocolate chip cookie, but I savored every moment of light when all I seemed to feel was darkness. It is my hope that this story of redemption will serve as a living reminder to you that life after emotional death is possible. Step into light, step into life, step into the hope that God has for you. Yes, you can.

2. I Need You to Just Trust Me

In between revelation and the arrival of my friends coming to my aid, there were minutes spent on the deep leather couch in the living room with my mom. Barely able to see through my tears, I asked all sorts of questions about what was happening. Why. How. When. What… My mom, through her own tears, said, "I need you to just trust me." My feelings were a swirled mess of wanting to trust her and questioning the validity of her word after the sudden shock of my dad's news. She had never given me a reason not to trust her, but then again, my dad hadn't either.

I chose to lean into her figurative embrace and trust that everything that needed to be revealed would be in due time. Knowing that she was also blindsided by the news gave me comfort. We were in this together- sifting through the information and processing it next to one another, in our own ways.

Trusting her meant that, for a time, my questions would go unanswered. Trusting my mom's discernment to reveal what was appropriate and necessary meant I didn't get the details I wanted. In the moments that followed and the times I asked to know more but was met with silence, I was frustrated. I felt entitled to know what had happened, to know the timeline and figure out when it was that I should have stopped trusting him. I drew the conclusion that my feelings of being wronged should be met with concrete answers, instead of vague statements to trust.

The following Sunday, my parents called a family meeting. After church Megan and I went to a friend's house and anxiously watched Netflix while my parents met with Heidi, Stan, and Dave, the head pastor of our church. It was 4:00. We arrived at home, preparing ourselves as best we could to sit down and wade through what seemed to be a murky future. I remember walking in and wondering if my dad would notice that my hair was different. I sat down on the couch across from his, with Megan on my right and Mom next to her. Stan sat next to my dad on his couch, with Dave in a chair next to him and Heidi in a chair between him and my mom. I felt uncomfortable looking around this awkward placement of musical chairs. Taking on the "issue" of silence as any people-pleaser would, I felt anxious as to how the conversation would go and how I would act. Even with the pressure placed upon me, by me, nothing could take my focus completely away from the small person before me. Once a pillar of a man, my dad sat pathetic and low in his portion of the room. His demeanor reminded me of the polyps in Ursula's garden in *The Little Mermaid.* He looked shriveled and weak, obviously in agony but trapped in the torture before him. Like the polyps, my dad's choices had led him to this place of pain when he trusted the liar of all liars and made choices that promised gratification but led to absolute destruction. Looking at my carcass of a father was too great a burden to bear. Where was the strong, righteous leader I had known? Where was the man that put our family first and made intentional choices for our benefit and success as a whole? How foreign it felt to look into the eyes of my father and see someone I had never known.

Heidi took our attention and laid out the expectations and boundaries for our time together. Our little miniature poodle, Charlie, climbed up next to me and laid down against my leg. Even our usually peppy pet felt the icy tension in the room and drifted towards us, finding an empty spot and just being there. I loved that about him.

When prompted, my dad opened a notebook and began to read a statement to us. Being a public speaker, he was used to this format of address. Being his family, this felt much too formal and all too foreign. In this moment of exposure, my dad revealed to us that he had broken his marriage covenant to my mom and sought outside their relationship for fulfillment. He read an apology and closed his notebook. Though I knew it was coming, the sting of the truth shot through me and my pulse bolted.

I had seen changes in him. I had seen new behaviors. In the months leading up to this explosion I had observed a switch and spoken up, but no changes were made. That being said, I felt bad for my dad. Looking at him in such a pathetic state was excruciating and I so wanted to wake up from this nightmare and return to the family of my childhood. All this remaining in my mind, I spoke up,

> "Part of me wants to forgive you, we all sin and I am no better. I can't help but think—how could we not be enough for you?"

I will never forget the look on my dad's face while I spoke. He looked as if he was on the brink of tears— deeply, wholly terrified. It's crazy that, in a way, I felt so proud of my response. My words were true. Even so, I was in the presence of important church people and felt like they should be impressed at what I said. This thought was affirmed when Heidi said,

> "Before we move on, Dave, I want you to hear what Maddie said—Your choices have put in her the notion that she is not good enough. You did that."

Megan and Mom spoke next and I truly have no memory of their words. I was too focused on trying not to cry and petting Charlie over and over, grasping onto the little guy that was still the same and not expecting anything of me. When there was a lull in the conversation Pastor Dave spoke up in a rough tone,

> "Well, Dave I have heard more compelling speeches at a City Council meeting!!! Show some fire! These are three of the most beautiful women in the world and you fucked up their lives!!! FIGHT for them!"

Without a word, tears flowed freely every woman's eye. We couldn't contain the emotion that came when a man fought for us, as my dad should have been. Sheepish and frustrated, my dad said,

"Well what am I supposed to do? I'm at the lowest point in my life, I'm a liar, they have no reason to trust me."

Dave jumped in, "Yeah but let *them* make that decision. That's not for you to decide."

It was shocking to hear, but even more, it was comforting and encouraging. While my dad focused on himself and all the reasons he couldn't speak up, Pastor Dave was focused on the destruction my dad had caused—instead of prioritizing our protection. It was affirming and soothing to see his righteous anger, and to know that we were not alone.

After this, I asked for specifics and was met with ambiguities. As frustrating as it was to feel simultaneously vulnerable, and buried in darkness, I am utterly grateful that I trusted my mom, though sometimes I was forced, and was not brought into the details of my dad's choices. The information I did know swirled through my mind and took so much time to process and come to grips with, I can only imagine how much more lost I would be if I had known more.

I think my mom's place in the beginning stages of our shattered family stands as an example of God's call to us during difficult seasons, whether intertwined with trauma or rooted in grief. We need to trust him. This trust doesn't account for fixing the problem or understanding what is going on, but that's ok. However, by trusting God we leave the details, solutions, and grip we have on our ideas of control in his hands, believing that he will take better care of us than we could ever take ourselves. This does not account for allowing yourself to be taken advantage of, or avoiding taking responsibility for your actions. I'm talking about mindful, intentional release of control to those with your best interest in mind, who, themselves, are giving control back up to God.

It can seem frustrating to walk in trust, as the act of submission often leaves problems unsolved and wounds open in pain. Trust, in itself does not fix the problem at hand, but refocuses our gaze to our unconditional companion. The beauty of trusting comes when what seems so foreign in the beginning turns into the best way of operating— though it takes some getting used to. Wounds left open are able to breath, be assessed, cleansed. Ultimately, when handled with care, these wounds can heal with minimal scarring. Trusting God in the middle of wild change leaves us capable of taking on our new reality one step at a time. Trusting that his process and timeline are immeasurably better than anything we could come up with is the first step in holding our pain with Christ as our companion and partner, bringing him into every aspect of our experience through honesty (More on trust in Chapter 4).

In the painful reality you are facing right now, what do you need to let go of and choose to trust God with? It can sound trite, I know, but the freedom that comes from releasing control is so crucial to the process of healing. I had to release details. I had to let go of the desire to know everything and trust that even if I knew everything there was to know, I could not fix it. Knowledge was not my savior, Jesus was, and I needed to act like it. This does not mean there wasn't pain or questions or fear. Like any muscle, I had to exercise my tendency to trust, I had to *choose* in every moment of anger and pain to give myself grace to feel, and release my need to know all things, because I would never get there.

When taking these small steps, it might feel like you're getting nowhere, I can so relate to that. When my goal was repairing my relationship with my dad, choosing simply to "let go" felt silly and irrelevant. However, as I learned in my first bout with deep depression, all victories are worth celebrating. Getting out of bed, getting coffee with a friend, taking a shower, cooking a meal...these seem like simple, easy tasks, but when trauma stomps on you, even these small steps feel like walking uphill. Give grace to yourself as you step into healing, notice and celebrate the victories as they come. Acknowledge the progress being made and do your best not to belittle it. You're doing better than you think and cheering on the small wins helps immensely. Not convinced yet? Well I guess you'll

have to just trust me…

3. God Can Handle Your Pain

Soon after my diagnosis of Major

Depressive Disorder, I went to college group

expectant of connection with peers, hopeful for

companionship in a time when I felt totally alone.

After worship we broke into small groups, reflected

on the message, shared our hearts, and prayed for

each other. As the night closed, I found myself still

in conversation with a woman named Sam. We

talked about school, work, and the ever-changing

lives we lead as single Christian women. I got
choked up talking about my relationship with God,
as it had become a struggle to connect and I felt
ashamed about my ability to relate to God, and
those that seemed to be close to Him.

Finally, I said,

"I just want to give God my best, He
deserves my best."

Sam replied,

"He doesn't want your best, He wants
YOU."

I grappled with this in the days following. I
was struck by just how off my view was. In a way, I
was right— He *does* deserve my best. Even more
though, I was mistaken in thinking I could ever
offer Him a perfect version of myself—on my own,
my best is absolutely unattainable. Coming to God
put together and wrapped up prettily is not only
exhausting, it's unnecessary. Have you ever had

someone dear to you act completely different than themself? Knowing them, you *know* how they operate and watching them try to be someone else is sad, frustrating, and sometimes annoying. This is how God feels when we come to Him pretending to be put together. When I try to present myself as anything other than the hot mess that I am—He *knows* I'm masking my mess. He *knows* all the little imperfections that I bring to the table and when I try to cover them, I'm sure it just seems silly.

What is the point of covering up thoughts and feelings when God already *knows* them? I am not suggesting that we throw reverence for God into the wind, but that we should bring our whole, messy selves into the presence of the One who knows us better than we know ourselves. Allow Him to be the instigator of change.

I left the conversation with Sam unsure of what it meant for me to bring my whole self before God, without trying to look or act put together. It's one thing to cry out to God in moments of crisis, but in everyday life when we feel like our worlds are settled, we can fall into the mindset that we must also be completely consistent in pleasantness and satisfaction. This "put together" facade not only takes away from our depth in relationships with people, but our ability to abide in God and learn from Him organically, naturally. When our focus is on results, not relationship with the Lord, the road becomes long, and the destination unreachable.

One of the best examples I can think of happened a couple years before my parents' split. When I was 19, I went to the doctor with what I thought was a spider bite. However, it quickly turned into an intense illness—an antibiotic-resistant infection that took over my body and had me on the couch without energy, breath, or motivation. I had boils all over me, my temperature soared, and at the deepest point of my pain I lost control of my breath and sight. I remember lying on my bed with the lights off and the fan on high. My dad sat next to me in a chair because I was too scared to be alone. My temperature was almost to 105, so we had cold, wet socks on my feet and head. I was terrified.

I breathed in and out, each one painful and difficult, slow and forced. My dad left to refill my glass of water and I spoke as loud as I could, though it came out as a whisper, "Jesus. Jesus. Jesus…" With literally all the breath I could muster I repeated his name and said, "Heal me." As I cried out to him, asking for deliverance, I remember the profound moment that my prayer switched to, "Jesus, *be with me*." The focus shifted from my healing, to His presence.

This changed everything. I still couldn't breathe and was unsure if I'd make it to see the next day, but I was sure of His presence with me, and that was enough.

This helped me see pain in a new way. Not only does God invite us to bring our pain, our frustration, our sadness to him, He steps into it. He doesn't look at it from afar and turn up His nose at the mess we're stuck in, He kicks off His shoes, rolls up His cuffs, and *steps in.* Not to take away the struggle. Not to even protect us from heartache or loss, but to be our companion, our partner, our ever-present help in times of trouble.

Isaiah 9:6a has always spoken loudly to me, and not just around Christmas time.

For to us a child is born, to us a son is given, and the government will be on his shoulders.

This brings to my mind a picture of strength, power, and might, wrapped in the gentle frame of a newborn baby. From compassion to conviction, the spectrum of God's character traits were and are embodied in Jesus. The physical brawn of Jesus, a man familiar with hard work, personified the pure power and might He obtained, and continues to obtain, as God in human form.

All throughout scripture we are given images of who God is through His interaction with those in His life. Not only does He accept those who come to Him—the bleeding woman, Mary Magdalene, the leper, the government official—He actively *goes* and embraces hot messes that aren't looking for Him—Hagar, Adam and Eve, and John the Baptist. If this isn't an indicator of God's ability and desire to know and have relationship with us, I don't know what is!

In the messy season of my parents' storm, I felt like everything I had ever known was taken away. The shaking of my family's foundation proved to be the first of many losses—followed by death, changes in school, church, work, friendships.

My therapist even moved away. Everything I relied on for security was Stripped away. I felt like a shell of a person—the very fiber of my being was being painfully manipulated and everything I had previously relied on in crisis had been stripped from me. My favorite relationships were gone. My ability to function was gone—my reality was gone.

Have you ever felt like this?

Has the foundation underneath you ever been shaken? or shattered? or Stripped from beneath you? Maybe you've faced rejection or betrayal that has shaken you to your core. Stripped is the word I use because it perfectly describes how I felt in its various meanings. Vulnerable, naked, open to further pain before restoration of any kind could be an option.

Though painful and often hard to see past, the state we are in after being Stripped is not the state we will remain in forever. Vulnerability is necessary. Emotional nakedness is necessary. Before the original beauty of anything can be restored, the layers of attempts to cover up marks of imperfection have to be chiseled away. In any situation, this process is painful, but when it happens in crisis it can also feel like punishment. I encourage you, friend, to lift your gaze beyond the pain before you and set your mind on the restoration that will be possible because of it. This is not easy by any means, and I probably would have rolled my eyes if I read this instruction during my season of being Stripped. Cling to the goodness that will be possible, even if you hold on to it with white knuckles and gritted teeth.

Because goodness, holiness, spiritual and personal growth—notice I didn't include perfection or even reconciliation—are by-products of suffering with the hope of God as your companion.

Pain is not scary to God. Pain is not foreign to God. He can handle it, and He can handle you as you walk through it. In fact, He desires to step into it with you, with every messy detail, every feeling of uncertainty you have for the outcome. He can hold the pain and He can hold you.

Let Him.

4. Message in a Salad

Some time after my parent's separation, I remember hearing a speaker at college group bring up the question, "What action do you need to take today to bring healing to your life?" We were instructed to sit in silence and meditate on this concept for a few minutes. While attempting to do so, all I could think about was the Bib & Bleu salad from Macaroni Grill. I had fallen in love with it a few weeks before and having skipped dinner on this particular night I was really hungry.

"Come on, Maddie, focus on listening to God, what step do you need to take?" I continued to sit there and repeat the word "Healing" over and over in my head—yet my thoughts were again interrupted with that dang salad! I shamed myself for the lack of spiritual focus a few more times, until a crystal-clear thought popped into my head—

Share a Bib & Bleu with your dad.

What? No. This salad thing can NOT be from God. I'm making things up. I'm hungry.

Focus, Maddie, come on.

Next came a mental image, some might call it a vision, of my dad, and me, and the salad. My chest began to feel hot and my breathing sped up. Could this really be the step I needed to take? Is it *really* on me to reach out to him when he was the one that royally messed up? Bitter, scared, and trying to trust that God was speaking and it wasn't just my growling stomach, I grabbed my phone and texted my dad. It had been months since we communicated and seeing his name on my screen brought physical tension to my shoulders.

I kept it short and sweet and said, "If you want to go to Macaroni Grill with me, I am available…" I didn't give in to my typical people pleasing behaviors. I didn't ask if he was available, and I didn't try to impress him. I extended the invitation and we made plans for that following Monday.

Monday night approached quickly and I found myself getting ready for dinner with my dad— I got dressed, put on my makeup and did everything I could think of to dress for success, in a hopeless attempt to mask my growling fear that this meeting would be just as hurtful as our last. I planned to get there early, sit, and have some bread by myself: home field advantage would be mine. I walked in, feeling safe in my plan to settle in before the betrayer came, but to my surprise he was already there, sitting on a bench, journaling. I began to shake and internally rolled my eyes; how dare he ruin my plan to be the first to arrive! He met my gaze and we were taken to our table. There was small talk, water refills, and polite order-placing, until the words came up and I couldn't stop them.

My dad said, "Thank you for meeting me" and in a blur of mixed sensations I let him have it, tears racing down my cheeks through it all.

"I don't want you to think that we're ok because we're not. Do you know what you have done to me? I can't focus in school, I feel weird in church... The guy I was dating—yeah, he stopped talking to me when he learned that I had 'daddy issues.'

You have seriously ruined my life."

I'm sure he apologized after that, but I was so

focused on not heaving out my suppressed breath

that I don't remember. I know he said,

"I want you to know that you can reach out

to me whenever you want, but I'll respect

your space and wait for you to contact me."

I flippantly tossed out, "Yeah well you need

to be someone worth reaching out to."

"I will really try to be."

"And don't think that me speaking to you

means I trust you because I don't."

For the first time in my life, I allowed

myself to speak my mind openly and honestly. And

I did it while speaking to someone that had done

immeasurable damage to me. I didn't justify their

actions with my faults or imperfections, I didn't

place the blame on myself, I didn't even worry

about how they would take my words, how they would be impacted.

I just *spoke.*

It was freeing.

After going through life with my head down, trying to make others comfortable, make others shine, I was assaulted by tragedy and I had some sense knocked into me. Honesty had been missing from my life and because of that, healthy communication was also lacking. In the moments of crying into my salad, I not only woke up to the power and necessity of speaking openly from my heart, even when my heart was battered and my words were aggressive, but my dad woke up to the true length of impact that his actions had created.

You've probably heard the saying "People will forget what you said, but they will remember how you made them feel." While this can be overused and dismissive, its core speaks to the importance of our actions, positive and negative.

I often forget that encouragement is not always flowery and uplifting. Sometimes, the encouragement that is needed is tough and rough around the edges. In the conversation with my dad, my words were encouragement, my tears were encouragement, and my painful honesty was encouragement for him to own his shit and get his act together. I wasn't telling him how amazing he was or what a role model he is, I was bearing my wounds and allowing him to see the damage he'd done, with the hope that doing so would spark action for change.

During our family meeting, when I sat with Heidi, Megan, and my mom, one point Heidi drove in hard was the necessity of our tears. As an emotional person, I was used to crying and feeling things deeply. But with the absolute rot I felt expanding in my soul, I wasn't prepared, or willing, to show any emotion to my dad. I wanted to punish him with silence and exclusion since our previously open and inviting relationship had ended in immense hurt. I wanted to lock down and show him just how out of my life he was—but that isn't what healing requires.

Our tears are precious, friends, and they are equally as powerful. If I had remained stoic, would my dad have seen the devastating weight of my pain he'd caused? Probably not. Would he have seen the change in me, the bruises he'd left on my heart, if I had not expressed my disappointment and lack of trust? Not likely. When facing people who have trampled on and tossed us out, vulnerability seems like the last thing we want to approach. However, small, safe doses, it can be a tremendous tool to usher in reality. I'm not suggesting you bare your entire soul—use caution—but allowing the wall to crumble allows communication. It gives glimpses into what is really going on in your heart, which can help reveal the real weight of their actions to the instigator of your pain.

Listen up, friend—emotions do not equate weakness. Your inability to hold it together while battling loss, betrayal, trauma, does not mean that you are not strong. This is a lesson that I am still learning. Although you are strong, your strength doesn't come from you, so you can't do anything to lose it. Your circumstances cannot change this. Your feelings will not either. Your outlook, however, has everything to do with how you embrace God's unconditional acceptance of you! I have always had the strength and the boldness of the Lord inside of me, but until this conversation with my dad and the divine salad, I embraced weakness in my words. I put fear in the driver's seat and allowed it to dictate how I spoke. Though at the time it felt weak and out of control, there was a moment where I became empowered, and confident enough to tell the truth. This is a hard switch to make when we are accustomed to shaming ourselves. However, by reframing our emotional experiences and emphasizing their strength, we have the power not only to change how we see the world, but how we interact with others.

By allowing our emotions to breathe, rather than suffocating them out of fear or shame, we embrace one of the most beautiful aspects of humanity. The extent of our feelings are not accidental—we were given a capacity for feeling by God himself. Everything you're feeling, everything you've ever felt—Jesus felt it deeper. From joy and contentment, to absolute rage and anger, Jesus has been there! This is one of the reasons Jesus came to Earth as a human. He didn't just come visit from

Heaven for a day, like a tourist, observing the wild humans and taking selfies with them. He stepped into humanity from the beginning and was in. our. midst. He was part of a family, part of a community, part of a nation. He did it all without sin, but His capacity for emotion was at human level, which gave him a perfect glimpse into every single struggle that we've ever encountered.

As I sat in my room, writing in my prayer journal during the worst season of my life, I came to a point where I wrote in messy, bold letters, "DO YOU EVEN UNDERSTAND?!" I now know—if there is anyone that understands abandonment, it's Jesus. When he hung on the cross, exhausted, aching, gasping for air, he was the embodiment of the sins of the world, and because of that, God could not be close to him. He cried out, "My God, My God why have you FORSAKEN me?" The Greek word here for forsaken is *"alman"* which literally translates to bereavement; discarded (as a divorced person) —forsaken (Strong, 488). The separation here was absolutely devastating. Though He knew the need for His crucifixion and resurrection, Jesus too cried out as He felt discarded and forsaken.

This gentle truth from the Holy Spirit was like a swift punch. I was gripped by the reality that the one I was crying out to does know the reality of abandonment, and where my relationship was with a human, His was with the glorious creator of the world. Even I had not felt forlorn in the way He did.

A new practice was needed in my life, as I desired to relate to God, but could not do so in the ways I had in the past. I longed to hang on His every word, but fought my thoughts as I read the Bible, feeling mocked in the Author's loving nature as I was feeling immensely unloved. As I searched for ways of reading and meditating on scripture, I found Bible journaling. This was the solution to my problem! If you haven't seen pictures of this, I encourage you to google it, they are breathtaking. Basically, Bible journaling involves writing/drawing in the margins of your bible, and meditating on the scripture you're articulating with art. I ordered a wide-margin Bible and jumped in feet first. With my colored pencils and microfine pens, I would read, find a single scripture to meditate on, and recreate the concepts to the sides of the scripture. This practice gave me a way to connect with God, which involved my brain and hands, and my love for creating.

I know it can be hard to relate to God when you feel discarded by Him. I know that no matter how much you believe in His goodness, the feelings of His cruelty in allowing you to experience suffering can be overwhelming. I want to encourage you, my friend, to think and pray about what your relationship with God might look like in this season. Allow yourself to dream, be creative, it might be wildly different from how you normally relate to Him. You are not "bad" for feeling distant, and more than anyone, God understands how you feel.

Maybe journaling is too heavy for you like it was for me, try listening to worship music on your ride to work. Maybe praying is too emotional for you right now, why not try meditating? These solutions can sound simple and churchy, but the way God speaks to you may certainly be different as you experience loss, trauma, suffering. When your normal ways of life look different, other pieces of life can start to look different, and that's not necessarily a bad thing.

Lean in to Him, friend, even if that means leaning in a way you've never tried before.

Lean in, and boldly remember that He is leaning in, too.

5. Tending the Wound

What was something that wove itself into your childhood? Good or bad, we all have common threads that touch multiple memories. A good amount of my childhood memories have to do with my severe eczema. I never really thought it was unique to have dry spots and open wounds all over my body, but kids around me made it clear with their questions and comments. I would scratch in my sleep, waking up to blood on my sheets and tears down my face, in tremendous pain. I tried every medication out there—steroids, topical and oral treatments, dietary changes, holistic efforts, everything. Thinking back on it now, I can't imagine what it was like for my parents to have to watch me go through it. They watched and did their best to help as I, a sweet little unaware child, tried not to scratch my endless itches, only to eventually break open my own skin to relieve the pressure.

Wounds are perplexing. Whether we fall off a bike or cut ourselves shaving, there are certain steps we take with almost every surface injury. Let's say I was at the beach and I fell against a rock, which cut open my leg and left sandy rock particles in my open skin. If I immediately put a band aid on it, and expected that to usher in healing, you would think I was crazy, right? Taking it a step further, if I tried to clean my wound but then did not bandage it properly, I would make a mess and get nothing accomplished.

Just like with physical wounds, emotional wounds

require specific, timely, orderly action, to ensure effective healing takes place.

Leave the wound open.

Wounds are painful! They burn, sting, and bleed, the list goes on. In the moment, it feels like leaving that injury open is going to end you. Taking no action can seem lazy or counterintuitive. But this is where vulnerability gives us a chance to breathe, to step into the light and honestly evaluate the situation. Sure, a temporary bandage might be required until it can be fully assessed, but we can't expect permanent transformation from temporary fixes. I know, I know, this part feels ineffective— It's painful, it's messy, but leave the wound open for a moment and see it for what it is.

In my situation, leaving the wound open meant that I trusted my mom, as awkward as it felt, and didn't try to understand everything. My soul was stabbed and bleeding, but I didn't rush to put pressure on it right away. I felt like my very life was being taken from me, but in this case, I needed to let the gash breathe so I could understand the trauma in its entirety. Only by doing that, was I able to see the reality and depth of the injury and tackle the triage from there.

Disinfect.

This is the most painful part of tending to emotional and physical wounds. To make sure the raw cut left open by betrayal, lying, or cheating, doesn't grow or become deadly, we have to dig out the gunk that could lead to future infection. While physical ailments require hydrogen peroxide or alcohol, emotional abrasions require brutal honesty and boundaries. Part of my personal disinfection process, and my family's, involved consistent therapy. I went every week. As each of us continued to go by ourselves, we also saw a family therapist, and my parents went together to a marriage counselor. In total, I was on a therapist's couch three times a week, and as a family we totaled weekly at seven sessions.

I cannot stress enough how vital this part was to our healing. Had we tried to jump into effective communication without dealing with our own shit, we would have skipped necessary steps, expecting impossible results. Yes, family therapy was helpful, yes couples therapy was helpful, but I found individual therapy most beneficial— because it was a safe space for me to be a masterpiece and a messy work in progress all at once. I believe that personal therapy is the best thing we can do for ourselves in times of crisis, and in my experience, it is a powerful tool that allows us to understand more about God and how he made us uniquely. My parents needed to dive into their own pasts and handle them before they could sit down with each other and work on their collective issues. This was all part of the disinfection process, and while it's a long one, it is vital if we want to get to healing.

Apply a healing agent.

My parents started using a new phrase while we

were going through the restoring process. When something was especially encouraging or comforting, they would say, "That is a balm to my soul." At the time I found it to be so cheesy and "church-y", but after being deeply cared for and held by my community in a new way, I understand what they meant. Find the balm to your soul. Find that friend calms your wounds and strengthens your resiliency. Jump into that activity that makes you feel fulfilled and excited. I often felt comforted by friends that would simply come spend time with me, watching Netflix or drinking coffee. This was incredibly simple and extremely helpful. When I needed to get up and *do* something, I enjoyed going to the gym, or taking my dog around the block for some time in the sun. Apply the healing agent that will enhance and further your healing process. As I have said in pages before, I know this can sound trite and overly simplified, but it makes all the difference. Be intentional and find that balm to your soul.

Have patience and leave it alone.

I got my first tattoo about a month after my reality crumbled. While my friends thought it was a cry for help, I had been wanting it for a long time and figured I might as well rip the band aid off and do it! I went by myself, played Tetris on my phone the whole time, and left feeling amazing. I had no problem leaving the band aid on, washing and applying ointment to it, and letting it heal on its own. My second tattoo, however, was a different story. I went to San Francisco for spring break with some friends and we each got a little tattoo on Haight Street. It was fun, a little impulsive, and one of my most cherished memories. While this one on my wrist healed perfectly, it was

itchy, scabbed way more, and took longer to

look beautiful! I wanted to take the bandage

off and be free immediately. When I hastily

tried washing it with fragranced soap I knew

I had messed up. It burned and I instantly

regretted touching it.

Leave. It. Alone. After you've done all you

can do, worked on your own shit, let the

wound breathe, disinfected, and slathered

that balm on, let it be. Just like touching a

wound won't make it heal any faster,

worrying about your emotional wound does

no good either.

It does not help our wounds to heal

when we blame the pain on the one who

caused it or try to punish them into

experiencing their own pain. When I'm

wounded, I want to destroy the person that inflicted my pain. In this case, my dad was the instigator, and when I sat in church, or was around people who thought highly of him, I wanted to scream at the top of my lungs, "He is a liar, do not trust him! He's not who you think he is!" I not only wanted to hurt him, I wanted to destroy him and leave him with nothing.

Equalizing our wounds does not make us heal faster. Destroying my dad's reputation would not have helped me move in the right direction. Shaming him further would not have helped his path towards healing, or mine. Our relationship would have suffered, had I been selfish and slandered him. Yes, I raged at times, yes I vented, but I did it in safe spaces —like therapy—with confidence, knowing that talking through what I felt in the right environment would lead to my betterment, not his downfall.

Being in pain does not give you the right to inflict pain on others. This was a hard concept for me to swallow as I stepped into life post-explosion. Just as I felt entitled to know details of my dad's actions, I felt entitled to slander him under the guise of my pain and feelings of abandonment. I thank God that He gave me the good sense to bite my tongue and think before I spoke. I thank God that He protected me from the consequences of my selfish desires. As I was finding difficulty enough in gripping small shreds of light and hope in my life, stepping into slander would have meant choosing darkness. I would have been hypocritically aching for healing as I tore open my own wounds. This is an essential, overarching attitude that fosters in healing, friends.

Your wound may have been inflicted my someone else, but it's tending to and healing is not their responsibility, it's yours. Your thoughts have power, your words have power, your actions have power. Don't tear them down and take yourself down in the process.

I love the words of Paul on this subject,

"Never pay back evil with more evil. Do things in such a way that everyone can see you are honorable. Do all that you can to live in peace with everyone. Dear friends, never take revenge. Leave that to the righteous anger of God." Romans 12:17-18

While he wrote these words in a different time, to a different audience, for a different purpose, the truth displayed here remains the same. Revenge, justice, and the final word is God's. Our desire for these things doesn't waver, but our grip on them opens when we understand that our patience and submission makes all the difference.

6. The Church in it All

The Church. This is a rough one.

Raise your hand if you've ever felt shamed

or degraded by someone that claimed to be living

for Christ. In the words of Michael Scott- One, two,

three, too many to count!

If you've been in the church (or you're human),

odds are you've felt less than at some point. This is

not to say that churches are malicious, but to point

out that as humans, we are flawed. These flaws can

present themselves even with the best loving intentions. I, too, have felt shame and inadequacy at the hands of a churchgoer, so I resonate with the pain that can be a sharp reminder of others saying you're not good enough… or rather implying it.

These kinds of experiences are why it can often be so extremely difficult to ask for and receive support in moments of crisis. If you're already feeling like people in places of leadership are looking down on you, then why would you reach out? Not only is this a devastating reality for a lot of hurting people, but it makes handling trauma harder, and perpetuates secrecy, which is often the root of the issue! Dear goodness. What are we to do?

As a churchgoer/ human/ person in pain, there are a few things you can do.

Remember what is true.

Start by working through the shame, pain, or inadequacy that has been placed on your heart, whether by you or someone else. All have sinned and fall short (Romans 3:23), which means that NONE of us are perfect, and we all require grace. If you find yourself comparing, feeling less than those that "have it all together," or are met with "should" at every turn, remember what is true—here in healing, truth sets the tone for heart, mind, soul. If I constantly put myself down, reading into others' comments, comparing myself, and calling myself unworthy, this will be reflected in how I live. I will go through life with my head down, trying to not burden anyone. What kind of a life is that? On the flip side, if I pause to remember that I am forgiven, I am loved, struggling, but I am not drowning, I will live like the resilient daughter of God that I am!

Truth will enable you to ask for help without burdening judgement resting on your back. Beginning any step of problem solving with an intentional mindset will bring what is important back into focus, and allow doubt, shame, insecurity, etc. to fade into the background—not totally gone, but not what you are looking to any longer.

By remembering what was true during my lowest season, I was able to lift my head, even if my body felt weighed down. Although I couldn't move myself out of the present situation, I could look up, look beyond it, and see the potential that could be.

Take control of your community.

Some of us have been blessed to be in strong communities which have carried us through crisis. This was my case, and I praise God for it. However, I have had other experiences where trauma hits and it feels as though I have no lifeline to reach out to. When these feelings occur, it is our job to grab the reins and take control of the community we have created. While meeting new people might be the last thing on your mind when your world is spinning, it does a heck of a lot more good than sitting at home, fostering discontentment with your circumstances, and complaining about how you have no friends. For some this might look like reaching out to old friends that were supportive in other times of life but have grown out of touch. For others it may be taking a risk and going to a new church/

community event/ networking mixer and simply being reminded that others share your interest and you are not alone.

Instead of reading at home, grab your book and sit in a coffee shop. Instead of listening to Sunday's sermon online, hop in your car and sit in the pews. It might feel awkward at first, you might have a meltdown, and you might not even get down your street before turning around. No matter what happens, taking small steps towards socialization can help your brain grasp social and relational connection when your life experience has crushed it.

I remember feeling extremely low at the crescendo of my college depression experience, which happened to overlap with my parental explosion. I got home from school and felt like a dark cloud— hovering around the house killing time before my therapy appointment. For the first time in my life, I felt millimeters away from physically harming myself and it scared the shit out of me. I reached out to a friend in my fear, and she said, "Go to Starbucks and just sit there until therapy. You don't have to talk to anyone, just sit." While my mind and heart were dealing with heavy realities that couldn't be healed by a trip to Starbucks, I found that my spiraling feelings of loneliness were able to be remedied by simple socialization, even just in the form of people watching.

When it feels like you can't do anything else, step out. Allow your body and heart to see and experience connection as you work to wrap your mind around it.

Give. Yourself. Grace.

This one is much less tangible, which is why we let it slip, but it is essential to our journey in the direction of healing. No matter what you are doing, where you are going, who you are with, you are *human* and as mentioned above, that means you will mess up. You'll say the wrong thing, you'll say nothing when you should have spoken up, you'll forget something, you'll make a mistake. And you know what? That is okay. It is. There are of course, places where reparations will need to be made, but in the grand scheme? It's ok. You have to give yourself grace. You have to learn to laugh at yourself. You have to stop "should"ing, and start letting things go. One of the ways I applied this concept was by intentionally decreasing the amount of times I said "I'm sorry" when it didn't need to be said. I would apologize for *anything* if I thought someone didn't like it. I had to intentionally learn to give myself grace to say something that wasn't perfectly received, while also learning how to grow in my confidence.

If you're a recovering people pleaser like me, you'll probably start this process by freaking out about the lack of grace you naturally give yourself. This is generally followed by a big pendulum swing to the "all grace" side with no consequences. As with any big change, you probably won't get it right on the first try. But guess what amazing opportunity this hands you? This allows you the opportunity to show yourself grace in the midst of your freak-out about grace-giving. This isn't a physical step but a mental and emotional one. Allow it to be a loving process, a sweet, gift to yourself that affirms the progress that you are making, rather than tearing down the distance you still have to cover. Celebrate the victories, as small as they are.

On the flip side of these painful, life-altering experiences, how do we, as the Church, support those that are walking through some of the hardest times in their lives? Churches have various groups, systems and procedures for helping those that are struggling, and as members of the body of Christ, there are quite a few options that we can choose from when we see people hurting.

Pray

Of course, this is a part of the equation, but we need to start looking at prayer as a vital first action, not a last resort. It is an honor, a privilege, and an absolute necessity that we step into the presence of God and bring before him those in our life that we know are hurting. Praying over those struggling around us is not done because there is nothing else we can do for them, it is because God is the only one that can know/love/help them in any and every way. As we submit those we love into the hands of God, over and over we recognize and emphasize God's power, goodness, and understanding of what's happening in their lives. There is no sweeter act of love and care, than sitting at the Father's feet, and laying those we love before him.

One of my favorite scriptures that a friend brought into my life during my darkest season was Exodus 17:8-15. I encourage you to read it and take in the beauty of this story in its historical context, and the overarching truths of God's character that it displays. Joshua is in the trenches, leading the Israelites in battle against the Amalekites, while Aaron and Hur are at the top of nearby hill with Moses as he holds up his staff. When the staff is raised, the Israelites excel, but when Moses lowers it, the Amalekites gain advantage. As you can imaging, this battle wasn't quick, and holding up anything for a long period of time would lead to fatigue. Moses becomes exhausted, and that's when his friends step in and offer a solution.

Exodus 17:12 says,

"When Moses' hands grew tired, they took a stone and put it under him and he sat on it.

Aaron and Hur held his hands up—one on one side, one on the other—so that his hands remained steady till sunset."

Think about this for a moment. Aaron and Hur didn't shame Moses for not being superhuman, they didn't call him weak or hold him to an unattainable standard. Instead, they stepped in and met his need. They physically supported him, and in doing so, stood with him in solidarity as he did what needed to be done for the victory of his people.

As my friend read this passage to me in our favorite Coffee Bean and Tea Leaf spot, I wondered where it was going. Yes, these are good friends, but in a season of broken trust and betrayal, how am I to expect anything good from people around me? She clarified her point and in doing so, spoke straight to

my soul. She said,

"They raised his hands when he couldn't.

They supported him and helped him

accomplish the task. Maddie, we are here for

you, on both sides, raising your hands. You

can't pray right now, you can't worship right

now, you can't even think of lifting your

hands right now—We're doing it for you."

This declaration was not one of forced

happiness or heavy expectations, but

assurance that in my lowest moments people

were praying, praising, and raising their

hands to God on my behalf. What a gift it

was to feel covered in prayer, at a time

where I could barely hold on to a thought

long enough to bring it to my heavenly

Father. For those suffering, and the ones

walking with them, prayer is powerful,

essential, and more impactful than we will ever grasp.

Reach out.

Simple, I know, but sometimes an acknowledgement or simple text message can make all the difference. If you don't know what to say, that's ok. If they don't reply, that's ok. Mindfully checking in on those wading through trauma and transition is a learn-as-you go experience, but to the person needing support, none of that matters. Sometimes they will be able to ask for encouragement or prayer, but in the depths of suffering and isolation that often isn't even an option. When you think about texting or calling the person that is hurting in your life, don't talk yourself out it because you don't know how they'll respond or you don't have the perfect words. Boldly, but tenderly, let them know they matter, they're on your heart, and even if they're far away they are loved.

This is something I'm working on implementing in my everyday life, as it is not just a principle for survival-mode or times of crisis. Reaching out, without expecting a grand conversation or huge recognition, is helpful for the person we reach out to, and our own ability to put ourselves aside and truly serve others. Many people reached out to me in my times of darkness, and although I couldn't always respond, whether because of my own forgetfulness or low capacity for emotional connection, I loved knowing that they cared.

What happens if they never respond? Or they don't want to talk? Or they are making decisions you disagree with? There are a few ways you can respond, but the following is my favorite:

Respect their boundaries.

Reaching out is so important and should be done in love, but when they don't reply for a while or don't engage with you in the way you would like them to, respect that maybe what they need is space.

There were so many kind people that reached out during my darkest seasons with words of encouragement, and while I appreciated their thoughtfulness, I didn't want to bear my soul to them.

This wasn't an insult or a put down, I just already had my circle of close friends in the trenches with me, and bringing more people in wouldn't have been helpful. I loved the sweet encouragements and compliments, but that was pretty much where it ended, because that was what was best for me. Most people had no problem respecting this, but there were some friends that I had to be more firm with. Not only were these conversations difficult because of their confrontational nature, but with everything going on in my mind and heart, I felt so ill-equipped. I was in no place to be initiating boundary-setting conversations, but when friends didn't respect that I needed our relationships to look different

while I processed the shambles of

my life, I had to draw a clear line.

This was painful for me, painful for

them, and an overall disappointment

because it could totally have been

avoided. Keeping your distance

might feel awkward or unhelpful, but

I can tell you from my experience

that in a season where my voice

didn't seem to matter, the friends

that listened to my requests for space

made me feel seen, heard, and loved.

And when I was ready for

connection and reached out to those

friends, they were ready and willing

to be by my side. There was no

questioning if they loved me because

they showed it in their actions.

Respect the boundaries, friends, and trust that when the time is right, you will be able to step in and help.

Triage and Offer Resources.

One Sunday morning in January of 2016, I woke up gasping for air, with intense pain in my chest. I caught my breath and figured it was anxiety, or asthma, but as the day went on I realized it was a much more serious problem. I checked in at urgent care and was immediately taken back to be looked at. Because the issues of chest pain and shallow breathing carry a higher risk for severe consequences, I was seen by a doctor before others that had been waiting much longer than I had. We found out that I had a spontaneous pneumothorax, also known as a collapsed lung. I was treated and taken care of swiftly because the possibility of further damage was much more likely than that of someone with a sore throat or sprained ankle.

If you've ever been in an emergency room, you have experienced triage. Whether you know it or not, your injury was assessed in relation to that of the other people in the waiting room, to see who was in most critical need of care.

It is my belief that we should approach emotional trauma with the same manner as the ER: through triage. By assessing the needs before us and tackling the most pressing, we are able to care in a way that lessens the chance of explosive consequences. One way my parents' small group assessed and met the immediate needs of our family was by driving to pick up my sister and bring her home on the night

everything changed. We would need meals

and therapy and all kinds of assistance in the

coming days, but our immediate need was to

be together. They started with what was

most important first.

Triage in trauma requires more than

one person can give, and that's ok, this is

where resources come in. Whether that's a

referral to a therapist, connecting someone

to a food pantry, or helping them find a

lawyer, take advantage of the people around

you that specialize in their fields. You will

not be able to meet all the needs of one

person, but you may know someone whose

load you can lighten or some small way you

can help them through it. If you don't know

where to start, reach out to your church or

community center and ask for their

recommendation. Point those in your life to people that can help, even if that means that you aren't involved.

One of the ways my friends supported me in this area was in helping me triage my needs. It would often seem like my world was swirling at high speed, and in those moments every need seemed like a vital one. By having their help in organizing the things that needed immediate attention and those that could wait, I was able to see my situation with clear eyes, through the perspective of my friends.

In all of these practices, it is important to remember that people are people, and God is God. We can do our best, but we can never expect to solve the problem or to heal the hurt on our own—whether we are the ones experiencing pain, or the ones walking beside those that are. It is an honor and a privilege to be used by God in the lives of others, but we must always step back and recognize that it is not our doing, but His.

Be the Church, friends. Have the hard conversation. Pray the big prayer. Feel the deep pain. Be the body of Christ, keeping Him upfront and in focus as you do. The Church goes far beyond the buildings we meet in or the denominations we identify with. Whether you care for someone through a time of praying over them, or a simple ride to the airport, all of the above principles can be practiced. This encouragement to be the Church stretches far beyond Sunday morning, and has room for flexibility and creativity in how it is applied. More than anything, ask God how you can do these things for the people in your life, in ways that meet their needs. There are few parameters on loving

people when crisis strikes, and that includes loving
people when you are in and outside the Church.

7. Beauty from the Ashes

Beauty from the ashes. It's cheesy, I know,
but the beauty that came from the absolute rubble
that was my reality is vibrant and indisputable.
When talking about the worst season of my life thus
far, it's almost laughable how far from it I feel. I
was telling my friend over coffee about some
memories from that first week, and I sat back as
silly joy bubbled up in me and I saw the evidence of
strides made throughout the past few years. Looking
back on the night my world crumbled and the

events that followed, a positive and removed perspective is the absolute last thing I would have expected to come as a side effect from the trauma we were dragged through. If you are in the thick of pain and loss and utter frustration, you may find this perspective difficult to believe or dramatically false. I completely understand this.

It is nothing short of glorious to look at my family today and see the work that has been done and the changes that were able to take place when my parents got their shit together. It took time. It took patience. It took vulnerability and courage and more firm reliance on God than I may ever be able to replicate. But the reconciliation of my parents is 100% proof of God's unconditional love, in addition to, not in spite of, His justice. This wasn't a flowery experience—it was muddy and excruciating. But as our family therapist said, "How do you get through a sea of shit? You can't go around it, you can't go above or below it, you just have to go *through* it." And through it we went. Many pages of this book were actually written across the table from my dad. The former instigator of my pain has become a new friend, as I have met and come to love a human I never really knew before. I have looked up while typing away in a coffee shop, and smiled at the craziness of God's love, the absurdity of His grace, and the benevolence of his sovereignty in knowing what was best for me, for all of us, in and through our deepest pain. My restored, or rather, resurrected relationship with my dad is nothing short of miraculous, and I am honored to see the display of God's goodness in my life.

I fully understand that not everyone's story ends this way. You may be walking through the deepest valley of pain you've ever been forced to experience, with no light peeking through, no glimmer of hope, no morsel of redemption in sight. Rest assured, and hear me when I say it,

God bringing beauty from the ashes of your collapsed world does NOT depend on reconciliation.

Yes, reconciliation is the goal when it's possible, but it's not always possible. Were you screwed over by someone with absolutely no concern for your thoughts or feelings? Were you abandoned by someone that vowed to love you? Were you deceived by the person you trusted most in this world? As difficult situations show us, we don't get to control everything. We don't always get a say in other people' actions. It's crushing and draining and infuriating, but reconciliation is not always on the table. However, I encourage you: do not let that take away from the beauty God will bring, because

He. Will. Bring. It.

Whether you get back together or not.
Whether they fall on their face and apologize or not.
Whether they own their shit or not. Your beauty,
your joy, your chance to flourish in the warm sun
when all you've known for months is the chill of
shade, does NOT depend on actions of the other
person. It depends on YOU and your choice to stick
with hope. Not forced forgiveness, not "having
faith" until you're blue in the face, not placing
unattainable expectations on yourself to get over it,
but authentic processing of the situation, and hope
that something, anything good will come from it.
Because it will.

This is not a flowery encouragement meant
to spring you into being immediately ok, but a shout
of solidarity that your pain is not for nothing. Not
only does God hear you, yes he does, but he will
use your pain and give it purpose. To minister to

others. To grow you into the person you were created to be. To show you how freaking badass you are and how much he adores you as his own. While pain is not his desire, sin and its consequences are not his doing, he takes the absolute worst and weaves it into something new, striking and impactful in its beauty.

Look at Joseph. Before you jump to the end of the story, walk slowly with me through his experience. From birth it was planted in him that he was special, he was loved, and he would make great strides for God and his people. He was encouraged in every way, given opportunities that his brothers were never offered, and held to a high standard of achievement. Imagine the attitude he would have had toward life—probably a little naive and immature, he soared through his days with everything he could ever need. He had loving parents, brothers who by all accounts were fulfilling their destinies as he will fulfilling his, and a strong sense of importance in his family and the family of God.

Can you imagine the utter despair of the betrayal he experienced? I imagine he was in disbelief at first, giving his brothers the benefit of the doubt because who could abandon their own sibling, their own flesh and blood! Thrown in a pit, left for dead for all he knew, with no way of escaping and returning to his life of comfort and excellence. And as moments, minutes, hours went on, can you imagine the shock his body would have been going through? I wonder if he felt like he was going crazy—I've certainly been there. And when light began to peek into this literal and emotional hole, was he filled with hope that this was just a sick joke? That the men he called family were back to save him? No, his days of misery were just getting started.

From there he was taken by foreign strangers, dragged (literally) for miles and brought to a land with new sights, sounds, smells, and languages. Everything that Joseph knew was left behind, including pieces of his identity. If you've travelled internationally, you can grasp some of what he experienced in those first moments in Egypt. I imagine he felt scared and small. With no one around to answer his questions, no piece of security to hold onto, we can understand the loss Joseph would have been feeling right about now. Maybe you've felt a version of it too.

For years he worked as a slave in the household of Potiphar, and when falsely accused of a crime he didn't commit by Potiphar's Mrs., he was imprisoned for *years*. Years! Can you imagine?

First, he was sold into slavery and abandoned by
his own brothers. I imagine his thoughts went
something like,

        "I guess this isn't so bad, I can get

      through this."

Nope. He's then dragged for miles and sold to a
new owner, forced to work in a completely different
environment, and learn everything as he goes.
In hope of this life treating him better than the dark
betrayal from his brothers, Joseph's thoughts would
probably go something like

        "Well I'm finally adjusted, Potiphar

        seems to like me and I'm moving up

        in rank, this could be a good thing."

Think again. In to prison he goes with no hope of
release, because no one in their right mind would
believe his word over the word of the official's own
wife.

When I think to this part of the story and put myself in that prison cell, I picture darkness and numb feelings of loneliness. How could God do this? Joseph was supposed to be big and knowledgeable and successful and instead he's in prison? I don't know about him, but I would certainly be questioning God's goodness, if I hadn't already done so.

I think that's one of the hardest parts about suffering—you can have so much faith in God's existence, but so little trust in his goodness. I remember writing in my journal about my frustration with God allowing my life to explode. I cried hot, heavy tears and grunted words as I wrote, "What the hell, God? Where are you? I know you exist, I've seen you work, I *know* you're good… maybe you're just not good to me." I ache for the girl I was. I do not have it all together now, but the restoration I experienced so radically is something that my sobbing, 20-year-old self couldn't even begin to fathom.

Joseph's time in prison allowed him to meet men that served in Pharaoh's court. And later on, when one of those men was called back into the ruler's presence, (and finally remembered Joseph's ability to interpret dreams), he told Pharaoh about him and Joseph was ushered into the presence of royalty. This gave him opportunities to work in close relation to Pharaoh, call the shots in some cases, and use his experiences and God-given abilities to save thousands of people from a cruel famine. How insane it is that God used the most horrific experience in Joseph's life to usher in restoration and provision for so many generations.

It is easy to overlook Joseph's struggle because we know how the story ends. It's easy to read scripture and roll our eyes and whine that it was a different time, God doesn't work that way anymore, or whatever we use to justify our lack of hope.

I acknowledge that not all stories end the way my family's has. Despite the circumstance, despite the result we longed for, we have hope for restoration, even if it's not relational, or in the way we expected.

Friend, beautiful reader of these pages— God has already written the end of your story, and it is a beautiful one. Take a step back from this tragedy, this trial you are in the middle of, and picture the restoration that could be. Put in your mind the image of total security in God's presence, because you already have that, whether your situation ends rosy or not. This is not to say that everything will end perfectly, that there will be no casualties, or that more heartbreak won't get in the way, but this is not the end of your story. The end of comfort, maybe, or the end of what you thought was your reality. This is not your end, but the beginning of unravelling the things in your past and present that are hindering you from grasping the fully realized version of who you were and are meant to be. Chiseling, peeling, stripping… These are all required steps in a new creation, and while they are painful, they pave the way for magnificent existence.

Choose hope. Choose beauty. Choose to believe that good will come, even if you have to grit your teeth and ball your fists and fight to get the words out. Make the choice that no matter how your world spins, how your life shakes and your body shivers, the grip you have on hope will not loosen, and from the ashes you will rise beautiful.

And you will rise beautiful.

8. A little help from my friends

You've finished the book! I hope it has been helpful as you step into healing after experiencing trauma. As you continue to put into practice what you've learned here, I want to offer additional recommendations to you, just like I would any friend that is walking your path. Here you will find a few of the many resources that have contributed to my healing, and I hope they will be helpful for you as well.

Books:

Emily P. Freeman, *Grace for the Good Girl: Letting Go of the Try-Hard Life.* 2011.

Henri Nouwen, *The Inner Voice of Love: A Journey Through Anguish to Freedom.* 1999.

Earl J. Henslin, *This is Your Brain on Joy: A Revolutionary Program for Balancing Mood, Restoring Brain Health, and Nourishing Spiritual Growth.* 2011.

Henry Cloud, *Boundaries: When to Say Yes, When to Say No, to Take Control of Your Life.* 2004.

Joshua Straub and Tim Clinton, *God Attachment: Why You Believe, Act, and Feel the Way You Do About God.* 2014.

Greg Boyd, *Letters From a Skeptic: A Son Wrestles with His Father's Questions about Christianity.* 2008.

Jen Sincero, *You are a Badass: How to Stop Doubting Your Greatness and Start Living an Awesome Life*. 2013.

Support Groups:

For struggles having to do with addiction, I strongly recommend finding a 12 step program, whether secular, religious, or one of each. Below are ways of finding them in your area.

Local Groups:

https://www.aa.org/pages/en_US/find-local-aa

Faith-Based: http://locator.crgroups.info/

Mental Health:

http://www.mentalhealthamerica.net/find-support-groups

Therapy/ Counselling:

I am a HUGE advocate for being counselled by a licensed professional. As amazing as our friends can be, they are often not fully equipped to help us

process fully, and it isn't their responsibility to!
Below you will find a few ways to locate therapists
in your area.

Secular:

https://www.psychologytoday.com/us/therapists

Faith-Based:

http://www.christiancounselordirectory.com/

If you are a student, I highly recommend looking
into your school's counselling center if they have
one. This is typically a very affordable way to get
help and not break the bank.

I hope these resources are helpful to you, and that
you find others that support you as well! While
reading and learning often felt like a fight, in the
delicate moments of my struggle I was more open
to newness than I normally would have been.
Because of this, the concepts and disciplines that I
learned throughout the pages of these books and the

conversations with professionals imbedded

themselves deep in my heart, and for that I am so

grateful. I hope this for you too.

9. Thank you Thank you Thank you

There have been so many people that contributed to my journey through hardship, and in my writing of this book!

There are countless people I want to thank—If you sat with me, cried with me, brought coffee or snacks or texted to check in during the darkest season, I want you to know that you contributed to my healing and I am so so thankful for you.

Mom and Dad—WOW. Can you believe this is real? Not only that we made it through that shit storm, but that we're friends? And thriving? And that people get to read about God's insane work through it all? I am so thankful for you two. For your strength, vulnerability, willingness to fight, willingness to be real… Thank you for listening, thank you for doing the hard work, thank you for reading this and seeing how it could be so helpful for others. I'm so grateful for this horrible season we went through, and how God used it to bring us closer to him and each other. Thank you for allowing our story to be shared, I'm so grateful for your hearts (and it's still crazy that I'm genuinely saying that!). As I tell everyone that asks about you guys, I like you SO much better now! Haha! Thank you for working on yourselves, working on your marriage, and setting a new foundation for our family to thrive. I love you!

Dave, Heidi, and Stan—Your comforting presence during the first week of darkness, and the weeks and months that followed was more helpful than I can ever express. Your kindness, strength, call to action, and vibrant truth telling (ahem, Dave) spun into motion the first steps we took towards recovery. I am constantly in awe of the ways God used you three to triage and treat so many of our wounds. Thank you so much for your intentional, delicate care, and the mighty ways that you held us, all four of us, in our explosive mess. You are the hands and feet of Jesus. You displayed the practical, need-meeting love of Jesus, and I pray that others facing similar battles have a trio of truth-bringers like you.

The Professionals—While I'd love to mention you by name, you know who you are. You three ladies walked with me through a storm I thought I'd never make it out of. While counselling is your profession, I see how you all went above and beyond to be my ally when I needed one. I felt unsafe and misunderstood in just about every area of life, but on your various plush couches throughout different offices, I could relax and know I was free from judgement. The coping tools I learned from you have carried me through many situations and seasons, and I am beyond thankful for your guidance and care. I truly believe with my whole heart that I would not have made it through the worst season of my life without you. I miss time with y'all, the warmth of your offices and safety of your presence, but I am so grateful that God is using you in the lives of others, and I had the chance to learn from Him, through you. Please read this when you struggle with a client- You made an incredible difference in my life, and you are undoubtedly doing so in the lives of others! Thank you so very much.

Ashley—My incredible editor! Without you, this would still be just a dream, taking up space on my GoogleDrive. Thank you for bringing your talent and care to something so close to my heart. Thank you for jumping on the vision and making it bigger and brighter. Your ability to understand my scrambled thoughts and turn them into something concise has made all the difference, Stripped would not be what it is without you. I am constantly learning from you, about language and life, and I can't thank you enough for believing in me, and this project. I love doing life with you, and this has been the icing on the cake! Thank you, thank you, thank you, dear friend.

MTPJR—My girls! From the moment I shared this dream with you there was nothing but support, excitement, and challenges to DO IT. Taylor, thank you SO much for the beautiful work you did for the promotional material, your talent is incredible, and I am so lucky to have it as a part of the launch process! I am so grateful to be doing life with you guys, you are gifts from God and this wouldn't be happening without you. Thank you for your constant supportive presence throughout this process and in my life.

TWIMW—You were some of the first people I voiced it to— Barb and Marianne, the first time I said "So I'm writing a book" out loud was with you in the pool so many summers ago! Thank you for your encouragement and willingness to help in whatever way you can. Shari, you have inspired me since we met almost ten years ago (crazy). Thank you, ladies, for building me up and bringing truth and light into this whole process. You constantly bring me back to Jesus and His purpose for my life throughout struggle and pain. I love you so much!

Caitlin—Thank you so much for your support and assistance through this whole process, dear friend! I loved learning from you and felt so encouraged to have someone that I could ask for help with writing, publishing, all of it. Thank you for sharing your wealth of knowledge, your heart, your apps and tools! I am constantly in awe of you. I cannot wait to see what God does in your life through your books and your life! Thank you for all of it, girl. Who would have thought that being in college together would lead to where we are now? So so thankful for you.

Beauty Loving Ladies—My ladies! I am so thankful for this life-giving group and how God has used you all to speak so clearly into my life. Your support and encouragement through this whole process has given me confidence and boldness to step out in obedience to God and get the dang thing done! Thank you for your love, support, and care. So very thankful for you.

25316365R00075

Made in the USA
San Bernardino, CA
11 February 2019